THE BOOK
New **Baptism**

The Rite of Baptism during Mass

The New Baptism Book

Published by **Redemptorist Publications**
Alphonsus House, Chawton, Hampshire, GU34 3HQ
Email rp@rpbooks.co.uk, www.rpbooks.co.uk
A registered charity limited by guarantee.
Registered in England 3261721.

First published 1975
This revised edition first published July 2012.
Revised and expanded August 2017.

General Editor: Denis McBride C.Ss.R.
Editor: Peter Edwards
Design: Eliana Thompson

ISBN 978-0-85231-390-9

Acknowledgements: Excerpts from the English translation of *The
Roman Missal* © 2010, International Commission on English in the
Liturgy Corporation.

English translation of the *Rite of Baptism for Children* © 1969,
International Commission on English in the Liturgy Corporation.
All rights reserved.
Confirmed by the Congregation for Divine Worship, 15th April 1970,

Prot. No. 1667/70

Concordat cum originali Paul Moynihan.
Imprimatur + Kieran Conry, Bishop of Arundel and Brighton
18 June 2012.
Permission granted for distribution in the dioceses of Scotland.

Printed and bound by John Dollin Printing Services Limited,
Whitchurch, Hampshire.

Contents

Parents and godparents

Parents have a central part in the Rite of Baptism. They present their children for baptism; they renew their own faith; they solemnly accept the responsibility of training their children in the Catholic faith. Godparents have an important role in assisting parents in the religious upbringing of their children, particularly by good example.

A non-Catholic parent

The Rite of Baptism presumes that both parents are Catholics. A non-Catholic parent is asked to join in the prayers and responses only in so far as he or she feels able. Don't fear you will embarrass anybody if there are times when you remain silent. All, and especially the priest, will understand.

How to act

Finally, nobody needs to worry about where to stand or where to move during the service. These details are left very much to the priest so that he may arrange them in the way best suited to the design of the church.

The Rite of Baptism during Mass

THE INTRODUCTORY RITES

All stand.

The priest comes to the altar while the Entrance Song is sung.

Sign of the Cross

All make the Sign of the Cross.

Priest: In the name of the Father, and of the Son, and of the Holy Spirit.

People: **Amen.**

Greeting

The priest greets the people in one of the following ways:

The grace of our Lord Jesus Christ,
and the love of God,
and the communion of the Holy Spirit
be with you all.

or

Grace to you and peace from God our Father and the Lord Jesus Christ.

or

The Lord be with you.
And with your spirit.

The priest or another minister may briefly introduce the Mass of the day.

Reception of the Children

The priest questions the parents of each child in these or similar words:

What name have you given your child?

The parents give the child's name.

The priest asks the parents:

What do you ask of God's Church for N.?
Parents: **Baptism.**

The priest addresses all the parents together:

You have asked to have your children (child) baptised. In doing so you are accepting the responsibility of training them (him/her) in the practice of the faith. It will be your duty to bring them (him/her) up to keep God's commandments as Christ taught us, by loving God and our neighbour. Do you clearly understand what you are undertaking?
Parents: **We do.**

The priest next addresses the godparents:

Are you ready to help these parents (the parents of this child) in their duty as Christian parents?
Godparents: **We are.**

The priest addresses the children to be baptised:

My dear children (if only one is to be baptised he greets the child by name),

the Christian community welcomes you with great joy.

In its name I claim you for Christ our Saviour by the sign of his cross.

I now trace the cross on your forehead(s),
and invite your parents (and godparents) to do
     the same.
Following the priest, the parents and godparents
now trace the Sign of the Cross on the child's forehead.
The Penitential Act is omitted.

Gloria

The Gloria is now said or sung on Sundays, except
in Advent and Lent, and on some other days.

**Glory to God in the highest,
and on earth peace to people of good will.**

**We praise you,
we bless you,
we adore you,
we glorify you,
we give you thanks for your great glory,
Lord God, heavenly King,
O God, almighty Father.**

**Lord Jesus Christ, Only Begotten Son,
Lord God, Lamb of God, Son of the Father,
you take away the sins of the world,
     have mercy on us;
you take away the sins of the world,
     receive our prayer;
you are seated at the right hand of the Father,
     have mercy on us.**

**For you alone are the Holy One,
you alone are the Lord,
you alone are the Most High,
Jesus Christ,
with the Holy Spirit,
in the glory of God the Father.
Amen.**

Collect

Let us pray.

All pray in silence for a short while, then the priest prays the Collect, a special prayer expressing the character of today's celebration. One of the following or another suitable Collect may be used:

O God, who bring us to participate in the mystery
of the Passion and Resurrection of your Son, grant, we pray,
that, strengthened by the spirit of adoption as your children,
we may always walk in newness of life.
Through our Lord Jesus Christ, your Son,
who lives and reigns with you in the unity of the Holy Spirit,
one God, for ever and ever.
Amen.

or

O God, who bring us to rebirth by the word of life,
grant that, accepting it with a sincere heart,
we may be eager to live by the truth
and may bear abundant fruits of fraternal charity.
Through our Lord Jesus Christ, your Son,
who lives and reigns with you in the unity of the Holy Spirit,
one God, for ever and ever.
Amen.

THE LITURGY OF THE WORD

All sit.

During the Liturgy of the Word there may be brief periods of silence for prayerful reflection.

First Reading

At the end of the reading, the reader acclaims:

The word of the Lord.
Thanks be to God.

Psalm

The cantor or reader announces the response. The congregation repeats it after the reader, and again after each verse of the Psalm.

Second Reading

On Sundays and some other days there is a second reading, at the end of which the reader says:

The word of the Lord.
Thanks be to God.

Gospel

All stand.

The Alleluia or Acclamation may be sung or said to welcome the Gospel. Then the deacon or priest says:

The Lord be with you.
And with your spirit.

A reading from the holy Gospel according to N.
Glory to you, O Lord.

At the end of the Gospel, the deacon or priest says:
The Gospel of the Lord.
Praise to you, Lord Jesus Christ.

Homily

All sit. After the homily there may be a brief period 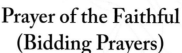 of silence for reflection.

Prayer of the Faithful
(Bidding Prayers)

All stand. After each intention there is a pause while all pray. This time of silent prayer may be followed by a response such as:

Lord, in your mercy.
Hear our prayer.

A selection of prayers may be found in Appendix A, pp. 30-31, or other suitable prayers may be used.

Invocation of the Saints

The Invocation of the Saints now follows:

Holy Mary, Mother of God,
Pray for us.

Saint John the Baptist,
Pray for us.
Saint Joseph,
Pray for us.
Saint Peter and Saint Paul,
Pray for us.
Saint N.,
Pray for us.
Names of other saints may be added.
To each, the people answer:
Pray for us.
All holy men and women,
Pray for us.

THE RITE OF BAPTISM

Prayer of Exorcism

The Prayer of Exorcism (of which the following is one form) and the Anointing with Oil of Catechumens prepare the children for the coming of the new life of God in baptism.

Almighty and ever-living God,
you sent your only Son into the world
to cast out the power of Satan, spirit of evil,
to deliver us from the kingdom of darkness,
and bring us into the splendour of your
    kingdom of light.
We pray for these children (this child):
set them (him/her) free from original sin,
make them temples (him/her a temple) of your
    glory,
and send your Holy Spirit to dwell within
    them (him/her).
Through Christ our Lord.
Amen.

Anointing

We anoint you with the oil of salvation
in the name of Christ our Saviour;
may he strengthen you with his power,
who lives and reigns for ever and ever.
Amen.

The priest anoints each child on the breast with the Oil of Catechumens, to strengthen the child with the power of Christ.

Procession

All now proceed to the baptistery or place where the baptism will be celebrated.

At the font the priest reminds the congregation of the wonderful work of God in the gift of baptism. He may use these or similar words:

My dear brothers and sisters,
God uses the sacrament of water to give his divine life to those who believe in him. Let us turn to God, and ask him to pour his gift of life from this font on the children (child) he has chosen.

Blessing and Invocation

Now follows the Blessing and Invocation of God over the baptismal water, of which the following is one form:

Father, God of mercy,
through these waters of baptism
you have filled us with new life as your very
   own children.
Blessed be God.

From all who are baptised in water and
   the Holy Spirit,
you have formed one people,
united in your Son Jesus Christ.
Blessed be God.

You have set us free
and filled our hearts with the spirit of your love,
that we may live in your peace.
Blessed be God.

12

You call those who have been baptised
to announce the Good News of Jesus Christ
to people everywhere.
Blessed be God.

(If the water is not already blessed):
You have called your children (child), N.,
to this cleansing water and new birth,
that by sharing in the faith of your Church
they (he/she) may have eternal life.
Bless ✠ this water in which they (he/she) will
  be baptised.
We ask this through Christ our Lord.
Amen.

(If the water is already blessed):
You have called your children (child), N.,
to this cleansing water and new birth,
that they (he/she) may share in the faith of
  your Church and have eternal life.
By the mystery of this consecrated water lead them
  (him/her) to a new and spiritual birth.
We ask this through Christ our Lord.
Amen.

Renunciation of Sin
and Profession of Faith

The priest addresses the parents and godparents:
Dear parents and godparents:
You have come here to present these children
(this child) for baptism. By water and the Holy
Spirit they are (he/she is) to receive the gift of
new life from God, who is love.

On your part, you must make it your constant care to bring them (him/her) up in the practice of the faith. See that the divine life which God gives them (him/her) is kept safe from the poison of sin, to grow always stronger in their hearts (his/her heart).

If your faith makes you ready to accept this responsibility, renew now the vows of your own baptism. Reject sin; profess your faith in Christ Jesus. This is the faith of the Church. This is the faith in which these children are (this child is) about to be baptised.

Do you renounce Satan?
Parents and godparents: **I do.**

And all his works?
Parents and godparents: **I do.**

And all his empty show?
Parents and godparents: **I do.**

Do you believe in God,
the Father almighty,
Creator of heaven and earth?
Parents and godparents: **I do.**

Do you believe in Jesus Christ, his only Son,
    our Lord,
who was born of the Virgin Mary,
suffered death and was buried,
rose again from the dead
and is seated at the right hand of the Father?
Parents and godparents: **I do.**

Do you believe in the Holy Spirit,
the holy Catholic Church,
the communion of saints,
the forgiveness of sins,
the resurrection of the body,
and life everlasting?
Parents and godparents: **I do.**

This is our faith.
This is the faith of the Church.
We are proud to profess it, in Christ Jesus
    our Lord.
All: **Amen.**

Baptism

Before the baptism of each child, the priest asks the child's parents and godparents:

Is it your will that N. should be baptised in the faith of the Church, which we have all professed with you?
Parents and godparents: **It is.**

The priest pours water over the child's head three times, saying:

N., I baptise you in the name of the Father, and of the Son, and of the Holy Spirit.

Anointing with Chrism

After baptism, the newly baptised are anointed with oil, a sign that each baptised person shares in the work of Jesus Christ. The priest introduces this as follows:

The God of power and Father of our Lord
    Jesus Christ

has freed you from sin
and brought you to new life
through water and the Holy Spirit.

He now anoints you with the chrism of
  salvation,
so that, united with his people,
you may remain for ever a member of Christ
  who is Priest, Prophet and King.
Amen.

The priest anoints each child on the crown of the
head with the sacred chrism.

Clothing with a White Garment

Each newly baptised child is clothed with a white
garment; if possible, one provided by the parents or
friends. The priest introduces this as follows:

N., you have become a new creation,
and have clothed yourselves (yourself) in Christ.
See in this white garment
the outward sign of your Christian dignity.
With your family and friends to help you by
  word and example,
bring that dignity unstained into the
  everlasting life of heaven.
Amen.

The white garments are put on the children.

Giving of the Lighted Candle

Holding the paschal candle, the priest says:

Receive the light of Christ.

A member of the family, or one of the godparents, lights the child's candle from the paschal candle. The priest says:

Parents and godparents,
this light is entrusted to you to be kept
   burning brightly.
These children (this child) of yours have (has)
   been enlightened by Christ.
They are (he/she is) to walk always as children
   (a child) of the light.
May they (he/she) keep the flame of faith alive
   in their hearts (his/her heart).
When the Lord comes,
may they (he/she) go out to meet him
with all the saints in the heavenly kingdom.

Prayer over Ears and Mouth

(This may be omitted in England and Wales.)

The priest touches the ears and mouth of the child with his thumb, saying:

The Lord Jesus made the deaf hear and the
   dumb speak.
May he soon touch your ears to receive his word,
and your mouth to proclaim his faith,
to the praise and glory of God the Father.
Amen.

Go to p. 26.

17

THE LITURGY OF THE EUCHARIST

All sit.

A hymn may be sung, and the bread and wine
for the celebration are brought to the altar.
The priest offers prayers of blessing.
If these are said aloud the people each time acclaim:

Blessed be God for ever.

The priest completes other preparatory rites,
then all stand as he says:

Pray, brethren (brothers and sisters),
that my sacrifice and yours
may be acceptable to God,
the almighty Father.

**May the Lord accept the sacrifice at your hands
for the praise and glory of his name,
for our good
and the good of all his holy Church.**

Then the priest says the Prayer over the Offerings.
One of the following or another prayer may be used:

O Lord, who have graciously gathered into
　　your priestly people
those you have conformed to the likeness of
　　your Son
(and perfected with the seal of chrism),
be pleased, we ask you,
to look upon them as acceptable sacrifices
and to receive them favourably
together with the offerings of your Church.
Through Christ our Lord.
Amen.

Open the door to your supper, O Lord,
for those who approach the bread that is
    prepared
and the wine that has been mixed,
so that, celebrating the heavenly banquet with
    gladness,
we may be numbered as fellow citizens of the
    Saints
and members of your household.
Through Christ our Lord.
Amen.

Eucharistic Prayer

The Lord be with you.
And with your spirit.

Lift up your hearts.
We lift them up to the Lord.

Let us give thanks to the Lord our God.
It is right and just.

The priest continues with the Preface, giving praise and thanks to God for the work of salvation. A selection of Prefaces may be found in Appendix B on pp. 32-33, or another may be used according to the season and occasion. Then the priest and people join together to sing or say:

Holy, Holy, Holy Lord God of hosts.
Heaven and earth are full of your glory.
Hosanna in the highest.
Blessed is he who comes in the name of the Lord.
Hosanna in the highest.

The people kneel.

The priest continues with the Eucharistic Prayer, which may be chosen from one of those in Appendix C, pp. 34-47. After the words of consecration he says:

The mystery of faith.
We proclaim your Death, O Lord,
and profess your Resurrection
until you come again.

or

**When we eat this Bread and drink this Cup,
we proclaim your Death, O Lord,
until you come again.**

or

**Save us, Saviour of the world,
for by your Cross and Resurrection
you have set us free.**

At the conclusion of the Eucharistic Prayer the priest
takes the chalice and the paten with the host and,
raising both, he sings or says:

Through him, and with him, and in him,
O God, almighty Father,
in the unity of the Holy Spirit,
all glory and honour is yours,
for ever and ever.
Amen.

Communion Rite
The Lord's Prayer

All stand.

At the Saviour's command
and formed by divine teaching,
we dare to say:

Our Father, who art in heaven,
hallowed be thy name;
thy kingdom come,
thy will be done
on earth as it is in heaven.
Give us this day our daily bread,
and forgive us our trespasses,
as we forgive those who trespass against us;
and lead us not into temptation,
but deliver us from evil.

Deliver us, Lord, we pray,
   from every evil,
graciously grant peace in our days,
that, by the help of your mercy,
we may be always free from sin
and safe from all distress,
as we await the blessed hope
and the coming of our Saviour,
   Jesus Christ.

For the kingdom,
the power and the glory are yours
now and for ever.

The Peace

Lord Jesus Christ,
who said to your Apostles:
Peace I leave you, my peace I give you,
look not on our sins,
but on the faith of your Church,
and graciously grant her peace and unity
in accordance with your will.
Who live and reign for ever and ever.
Amen.

The peace of the Lord be with you always.
And with your spirit.

Let us offer each other the sign of peace.

All offer one another the customary sign of peace,
which is an expression of peace, communion
and charity.

The Breaking of the Bread

The priest takes the host and breaks it, as the
following is sung or said:

**Lamb of God, you take away the sins of the world,
have mercy on us.**

**Lamb of God, you take away the sins of the world,
have mercy on us.**

**Lamb of God, you take away the sins of the world,
grant us peace.**

Invitation to Communion

The people kneel.
The priest raises the host and says:

Behold the Lamb of God,
behold him who takes away the sins of
   the world.
Blessed are those called to the supper of
   the Lamb.

**Lord, I am not worthy
that you should enter under my roof,
but only say the word
and my soul shall be healed.**

After the priest has consumed the Body and Blood of
Christ, the communicants come forward
in reverent procession to receive Communion. The
Communion Antiphon may be said or sung, or a
hymn or psalm may be sung. The priest
or minister shows the host to each of the
communicants, saying:

The Body of Christ.
Amen.

When Communion is ministered under both kinds,
the minister of the chalice raises it slightly and
shows it to each of the communicants, saying:

The Blood of Christ.
Amen.

After the distribution of Communion, if appropriate,
a silence may be observed for a while, or a psalm or
other canticle of praise or a hymn may be sung.
Then the priest says:

Let us pray.

All stand and pray in silence. Then the priest says
the Prayer after Communion. One of the following
or another prayer may be used.

Grant, O Lord, we pray,
that, nourished with the Sacrament of your
   Son's Body and Blood,
we may grow in the communion of his Spirit
and in love for one another,
and so, through ardent charity,
reach the full stature of the Body of Christ.
Who lives and reigns for ever and ever.
Amen.

or

Grant, O Lord,
that by the power of this Sacrament
we, who have proclaimed in celebration
the glorious mystery of your Son's Death and
   Resurrection,
may also profess it by our manner of life.
Through Christ our Lord.
Amen.

THE CONCLUDING RITES

 Any brief announcements now follow.
The Lord be with you.
And with your spirit.

Blessing

The priest now gives the blessing, in the following or another form.
The priest blesses the mothers, who hold their children in their arms:

(If more than one child has been baptised):

God the Father,
through his Son, the Virgin Mary's child,
has brought joy to all Christian mothers,
as they see the hope of eternal life shine on
    their children.
May he bless the mothers of these children.
They now thank God for the gift of their
    children.
May they be one with them in thanking God
    for ever in heaven,
in Christ Jesus our Lord.
Amen.

 (If only one child has been baptised):
God the Father,
through his Son, the Virgin Mary's child,
has brought joy to all Christian mothers,
as they see the hope of eternal life shine on
    their children.

May he bless the mother of this child.
She now thanks God for the gift of her child.
May she be one with her child in thanking God
  for ever in heaven,
in Christ Jesus our Lord.
Amen.

He then blesses the fathers:

(If more than one child has been baptised):

God is the giver of all life, human and divine.
May he bless the fathers of these children.
With their wives they will be the first teachers
  of their children
in the ways of faith.
May they also be the best of teachers,
bearing witness to the faith
by what they say and do,
in Christ Jesus our Lord.
Amen.

(If only one child has been baptised):

God is the giver of all life, human and divine.
May he bless the father of this child.
He and his wife will be the first teachers of
  their child
in the ways of faith.
May they also be the best of teachers,
bearing witness to the faith
by what they say and do,
in Christ Jesus our Lord.
Amen.

Lastly he blesses the entire assembly in a form such as the following:

By God's gift, through water and the Holy Spirit,
we are reborn to everlasting life.
In his goodness,
may he continue to pour out his blessings
    upon all present
who are his sons and daughters.
May he make them always,
wherever they may be,
faithful members of his holy people.
May he send his peace upon all who are
    gathered here,
in Christ Jesus our Lord.
Amen.

May almighty God bless you,
the Father, and the Son, ✠ and the Holy Spirit.
Amen.

Then the deacon or the priest says:
Go forth, the Mass is ended.

or

Go and announce the Gospel of the Lord.

or

Go in peace, glorifying the Lord by your life.

or

Go in peace.
Thanks be to God.

A hymn may be sung.

28

Appendix A

Prayer of the Faithful
(Bidding Prayers)

Priest: My brothers and sisters,
let us ask our Lord Jesus Christ
to look lovingly on these children who are (this
    child who is) to be baptised,
on their (his/her) parents and godparents,
and on all the baptised.

Reader: By the mystery of your death and
    resurrection,
bathe these children (this child) in light,
give them (him/her) the new life of baptism
and welcome them (him/her) into your holy
    Church.
Lord, hear us.
Lord, graciously hear us.

Through baptism and confirmation,
make them (him/her) your faithful follower(s)
and witnesses (a witness) to your Gospel.
Lord, hear us.
Lord, graciously hear us.

Lead them (him/her) by a holy life to the joys
  of God's kingdom.
Lord, hear us.
Lord, graciously hear us.

Make the lives of their (his/her) parents and
  godparents
examples of faith to inspire these children
  (this child).
Lord, hear us.
Lord, graciously hear us.

Keep their families (his/her family) always in
  your love.
Lord, hear us.
Lord, graciously hear us.

Renew the grace of our baptism in each one of us.
Lord, hear us.
Lord, graciously hear us.

Appendix B
Prefaces

During the Easter season:

It is truly right and just, our duty and our
    salvation,
at all times to acclaim you, O Lord,
but in this time above all to laud you yet more
    gloriously,
when Christ our Passover has been sacrificed.

Through him the children of light rise to
    eternal life
and the halls of the heavenly Kingdom
are thrown open to the faithful;
for his Death is our ransom from death,
and in his rising the life of all has risen.

Therefore, overcome with paschal joy,
every land, every people exults in your praise
and even the heavenly Powers, with the angelic
    hosts,
sing together the unending hymn of your glory,
    as they acclaim:

Holy, Holy, Holy Lord God of hosts...

It is truly right and just, our duty and our
    salvation,
always and everywhere to give you thanks,
Lord, holy Father, almighty and eternal God,
through Christ our Lord.

For through his Paschal Mystery,
he accomplished the marvellous deed,
by which he has freed us from the yoke of sin
    and death,
summoning us to the glory of being now called
a chosen race, a royal priesthood,
a holy nation, a people for your own
    possession,
to proclaim everywhere your mighty works,
for you have called us out of darkness
into your own wonderful light.

And so, with Angels and Archangels,
with Thrones and Dominions,
and with all the hosts and Powers of heaven,
we sing the hymn of your glory,
as without end we acclaim:

Holy, Holy, Holy Lord God of hosts...

Appendix C
Eucharistic Prayers

Eucharistic Prayer I
(The Roman Canon)

Kneel.

To you, therefore, most merciful Father,
we make humble prayer and petition
through Jesus Christ, your Son, our Lord:
that you accept
and bless ✠ these gifts, these offerings,
these holy and unblemished sacrifices,
which we offer you firstly
for your holy catholic Church.
Be pleased to grant her peace,
to guard, unite and govern her
throughout the whole world,
together with your servant N. our Pope
and N. our Bishop,
and all those who, holding to the truth,
hand on the catholic and apostolic faith.

Remember, Lord, your servants
who have presented your chosen ones
for the holy grace of your Baptism,

Here the names of the godparents are read out.

and all gathered here,
whose faith and devotion are known to you.
For them, we offer you this sacrifice of praise

or they offer it for themselves
and all who are dear to them:
for the redemption of their souls,
in hope of health and well-being,
and paying their homage to you,
the eternal God, living and true.

In communion with those whose memory we
    venerate,
especially the glorious ever-Virgin Mary,
Mother of our God and Lord, Jesus Christ,
*and blessed Joseph, her Spouse,
your blessed Apostles and Martyrs,
Peter and Paul, Andrew,
(James, John,
Thomas, James, Philip,
Bartholomew, Matthew,
Simon and Jude;
Linus, Cletus, Clement, Sixtus,
Cornelius, Cyprian,
Lawrence, Chrysogonus,
John and Paul,
Cosmas and Damian)
and all your Saints;
we ask that through their merits and prayers,
in all things we may be defended
by your protecting help.
(Through Christ our Lord. Amen.)

Therefore, Lord, we pray:
graciously accept this oblation of our service,
that of your whole family,
which we offer you
also for those to whom you have been pleased
    to give
the new birth of water and the Holy Spirit,
granting them forgiveness of all their sins
so as to find them in Christ Jesus our Lord;
and command that their names be written
in the book of the living.
(Through Christ our Lord. Amen.)

Be pleased, O God, we pray,
to bless, acknowledge,
and approve this offering in every respect;
make it spiritual and acceptable,
so that it may become for us
the Body and Blood of your most beloved Son,
our Lord Jesus Christ.

On the day before he was to suffer,
he took bread in his holy and venerable hands,
and with eyes raised to heaven
to you, O God, his almighty Father,
giving you thanks, he said the blessing,
broke the bread
and gave it to his disciples, saying:

Take this, all of you, and eat of it,
for this is my Body,
which will be given up for you.

In a similar way, when supper was ended,
he took this precious chalice
in his holy and venerable hands,
and once more giving you thanks, he said the
    blessing
and gave the chalice to his disciples, saying:

Take this, all of you, and drink from it,
for this is the chalice of my Blood,
the Blood of the new and eternal
    covenant,
which will be poured out for you and for
    many
for the forgiveness of sins.

Do this in memory of me.

The mystery of faith.

**We proclaim your Death, O Lord,
and profess your Resurrection
until you come again.**

or

**When we eat this Bread and drink this Cup,
we proclaim your Death, O Lord,
until you come again.**

or

**Save us, Saviour of the world,
for by your Cross and Resurrection
you have set us free.**

Therefore, O Lord,
as we celebrate the memorial of the blessed Passion,
the Resurrection from the dead,
and the glorious Ascension into heaven
of Christ, your Son, our Lord,
we, your servants and your holy people,
offer to your glorious majesty
from the gifts that you have given us,
this pure victim,
this holy victim,
this spotless victim,
the holy Bread of eternal life
and the Chalice of everlasting salvation.

Be pleased to look upon these offerings
with a serene and kindly countenance,
and to accept them,
as once you were pleased to accept
the gifts of your servant Abel the just,
the sacrifice of Abraham, our father in faith,
and the offering of your high priest Melchizedek,
a holy sacrifice, a spotless victim.

In humble prayer we ask you, almighty God:
command that these gifts be borne
by the hands of your holy Angel
to your altar on high
in the sight of your divine majesty,
so that all of us, who through this
    participation at the altar

receive the most holy Body and Blood of
    your Son,
may be filled with every grace and heavenly
    blessing.
(Through Christ our Lord. Amen.)

Remember also, Lord, your servants N. and N.,
who have gone before us with the sign of
    faith
and rest in the sleep of peace.
Grant them, O Lord, we pray,
and all who sleep in Christ,
a place of refreshment, light and peace.
(Through Christ our Lord. Amen.)

To us, also, your servants, who, though
    sinners,
hope in your abundant mercies,
graciously grant some share
and fellowship with your holy Apostles and
    Martyrs:
with John the Baptist, Stephen,
Matthias, Barnabas,
(Ignatius, Alexander,
Marcellinus, Peter,
Felicity, Perpetua,
Agatha, Lucy,
Agnes, Cecilia, Anastasia)
and all your Saints;
admit us, we beseech you,

into their company,
not weighing our merits,
but granting us your pardon,
through Christ our Lord.

Through whom
you continue to make all these good things,
    O Lord;
you sanctify them, fill them with life,
bless them, and bestow them upon us.

Through him, and with him, and in him,
O God, almighty Father,
in the unity of the Holy Spirit,
all glory and honour is yours,
for ever and ever.
Amen.

Then follows the Communion Rite, p. 22.

Eucharistic Prayer II

Kneel.

You are indeed Holy, O Lord,
the fount of all holiness.
Make holy, therefore, these gifts, we pray,
by sending down your Spirit upon them like
   the dewfall,
so that they may become for us
the Body and ✠ Blood of our Lord, Jesus Christ.

At the time he was betrayed
and entered willingly into his Passion,
he took bread and, giving thanks, broke it,
and gave it to his disciples, saying:

TAKE THIS, ALL OF YOU, AND EAT OF IT,
FOR THIS IS MY BODY,
WHICH WILL BE GIVEN UP FOR YOU.

In a similar way, when supper was ended,
he took the chalice
and, once more giving thanks,
he gave it to his disciples, saying:

TAKE THIS, ALL OF YOU, AND DRINK FROM IT,
FOR THIS IS THE CHALICE OF MY BLOOD,
THE BLOOD OF THE NEW AND ETERNAL
   COVENANT,
WHICH WILL BE POURED OUT FOR YOU AND FOR
   MANY
FOR THE FORGIVENESS OF SINS.

DO THIS IN MEMORY OF ME.

The mystery of faith.

We proclaim your Death, O Lord,
and profess your Resurrection
until you come again.

or

When we eat this Bread and drink this Cup,
we proclaim your Death, O Lord,
until you come again.

or

Save us, Saviour of the world,
for by your Cross and Resurrection
you have set us free.

Therefore, as we celebrate
the memorial of his Death and Resurrection,
we offer you, Lord,
the Bread of life and the Chalice of salvation,
giving thanks that you have held us worthy
to be in your presence and minister to you.

Humbly we pray
that, partaking of the Body and Blood of Christ,
we may be gathered into one by the Holy Spirit.

Remember, Lord, your Church,
spread throughout the world,
and bring her to the fullness of charity,
together with N. our Pope and N. our Bishop
and all the clergy.

Remember also, Lord, the newly baptised
who, through Baptism (and Confirmation),
have today been joined to your family,
that they may follow Christ, your Son,
with a generous heart and a willing spirit.

Remember also our brothers and sisters
who have fallen asleep in the hope of the
    resurrection,
and all who have died in your mercy:
welcome them into the light of your face.
Have mercy on us all, we pray,
that with the Blessed Virgin Mary, Mother
    of God,
with blessed Joseph, her Spouse,
with the blessed Apostles,
and all the Saints who have pleased you
    throughout the ages,
we may merit to be coheirs to eternal life,
and may praise and glorify you
through your Son, Jesus Christ.

Through him, and with him, and in him,
O God, almighty Father,
in the unity of the Holy Spirit,
all glory and honour is yours,
for ever and ever.
Amen.

Then follows the Communion Rite, p. 22.

Eucharistic Prayer III

Kneel.

You are indeed Holy, O Lord,
and all you have created
rightly gives you praise,
for through your Son our Lord Jesus Christ,
by the power and working of the Holy Spirit,
you give life to all things and make them holy,
and you never cease to gather a people to
  yourself,
so that from the rising of the sun to its setting
a pure sacrifice may be offered to your name.

Therefore, O Lord, we humbly implore you:
by the same Spirit graciously make holy
these gifts we have brought to you for
  consecration,
that they may become the Body and ✠ Blood
of your Son our Lord Jesus Christ,
at whose command we celebrate these mysteries.

For on the night he was betrayed
he himself took bread,
and giving you thanks, he said the blessing,
broke the bread and gave it to his disciples,
  saying:

TAKE THIS, ALL OF YOU, AND EAT OF IT,
FOR THIS IS MY BODY,
WHICH WILL BE GIVEN UP FOR YOU.

In a similar way, when supper was ended,
he took the chalice,

and giving you thanks, he said the blessing,
and gave the chalice to his disciples, saying:

TAKE THIS, ALL OF YOU, AND DRINK FROM IT,
FOR THIS IS THE CHALICE OF MY BLOOD,
THE BLOOD OF THE NEW AND ETERNAL
  COVENANT,
WHICH WILL BE POURED OUT FOR YOU AND FOR
  MANY
FOR THE FORGIVENESS OF SINS.

DO THIS IN MEMORY OF ME.

The mystery of faith.

**We proclaim your Death, O Lord,
and profess your Resurrection
until you come again.**

or

**When we eat this Bread and drink this Cup,
we proclaim your Death, O Lord,
until you come again.**

or

**Save us, Saviour of the world,
for by your Cross and Resurrection
you have set us free.**

Therefore, O Lord, as we celebrate the memorial
of the saving Passion of your Son,
his wondrous Resurrection
and Ascension into heaven,
and as we look forward to his second coming,
we offer you in thanksgiving
this holy and living sacrifice.

Look, we pray, upon the oblation of your Church
and, recognising the sacrificial Victim by whose
    death
you willed to reconcile us to yourself,
grant that we, who are nourished
by the Body and Blood of your Son
and filled with his Holy Spirit,
may become one body, one spirit in Christ.

May he make of us
an eternal offering to you,
so that we may obtain an inheritance with
    your elect,
especially with the most Blessed Virgin Mary,
    Mother of God,
with blessed Joseph, her Spouse,
with your blessed Apostles and glorious Martyrs
(with Saint N.: the Saint of the day or Patron Saint)
and with all the Saints,
on whose constant intercession in your presence
we rely for unfailing help.

May this Sacrifice of our reconciliation,
we pray, O Lord,
advance the peace and salvation of all the world.
Be pleased to confirm in faith and charity
your pilgrim Church on earth,
with your servant N. our Pope and N. our Bishop,
the Order of Bishops, all the clergy,
and the entire people you have gained for
    your own.

Listen graciously to the prayers of this family,
whom you have summoned before you.
Strengthen, we pray, in their holy purpose
your servants who by the cleansing waters of
    rebirth
(and the bestowing of the Holy Spirit)
have today been joined to your people,
and grant that they may always walk in
    newness of life.
In your compassion, O merciful Father,
gather to yourself all your children
scattered throughout the world.

To our departed brothers and sisters
and to all who were pleasing to you
at their passing from this life,
give kind admittance to your kingdom.
There we hope to enjoy for ever the fullness of
    your glory
through Christ our Lord,
through whom you bestow on the world all that
is good.

Through him, and with him, and in him,
O God, almighty Father,
in the unity of the Holy Spirit,
all glory and honour is yours,
for ever and ever.
Amen.

Then follows the Communion Rite, p. 22.